In Tune

PIONEER EDITION

By Susan Blackaby

CONTENTS

Music & Culture
IN HARMONY

By Susan Blackaby

How old is music? No one knows. Some say it is as old as time. Ask the early people in Australia. They say music started when the world began. Their oldest **songs** tell how singing made the universe. Hopi stories tell about Spider Woman. She sang a song to bring the first people to life.

Long ago, people thought music made the universe run smoothly.

People in all cultures make music. People play pipes. They twang strings. They thump drums and clap hands. They hum tunes. They chant verses. They sing out strong. Music is shared by people all over the world.

Singing in History

Which came first—singing or speaking? The answer could be singing! Speaking may have come much later. Once people started to sing, they needed **instruments**, too. They made drums and harps. They made lutes and flutes. These instruments of long ago are still used today.

All cultures sing. These days, people make music for fun. In the past, it was a big part of daily life. Singers reported the news. They told stories. They shared information. They kept records. Many people did not have a way to write things down. Singers had to keep track of details.

Remembering the Past

In some cultures, leaders hired people to sing. They were called praise singers. They sang about the leaders' brave deeds. They sang about battles of the past. They sang about family **history**. They sang about laws and rules. Praise singers told and retold old stories. Their songs kept these traditions going.

In many places, singers still keep track of facts. In West Africa, a person called a *griot* (GREE-oh) sings about history. In Australia, singers use songs to tell old stories. They use songs to report new experiences, too. And they use songs to teach lessons about right and wrong.

Music School. *This is part of a cup from ancient Greece. It shows a school where boys learn to play instruments.*

Sharing Ideas

Music can bring people together. People who live in the same place sing the same folk tunes. Singing helps them share traditions. Millions of people who live in the same country sing the same national anthem. It is a song that shows pride and respect.

People listen to music. They play instruments. They sing together. Music links people to the past. When people move from place to place, they take tunes and dance steps with them.

Music helps people hold on to cultural ties. It helps them stay connected to old places. It also can help them share their culture with new friends.

In many cultures, people are not free. They are not given a chance to speak. But their singing cannot be stopped. People sing about hard times. Singing together can give people hope. Singing together can make people feel brave.

Songs to Celebrate. *Women from Kenya sing together in traditional clothes.*

Working in Tune

In many cultures, people sing while they work. Singing helps them get their jobs done.

Lots of work songs have a call-and-response **pattern**. The leader calls out a line. Then the rest of the singers answer. The answer may repeat part of the call.

Call: Won't you ring, old hammer?

Response: Hammer, ring.

Call: Won't you ring, old hammer?

Response: Hammer, ring.

Call: Broke the handle on my hammer,

Response: Hammer, ring.

Call: Broke the handle on my hammer,

Response: Hammer, ring.

Work Song. *Men in Egypt sing as they dig. The man in blue leads the song.*

Raised Voices, Raised Awareness

AFRICA

Mozambique

Niassa is in Mozambique. It is a very poor place. For years and years, the people there have had no hope. They cannot meet their needs. They do not have clean drinking water. They do not have food to eat.

Feliciano dos Santos is from Niassa. He is a National Geographic Emerging Explorer. He plays music all over the world. Santos could have used his fame to get out of Niassa. Instead, he is using it to help.

Traditional Tunes, New Ideas

Feliciano dos Santos makes people think. He sings folk tunes that people have heard. They know the beat of the drums. But the words he sings are new!

As a child, Feliciano dos Santos had polio. Polio is a disease. It can be spread by dirty water. Santos wants to stop diseases like polio. He sings about healthy habits. He sings about clean water. He sings about taking care of waste and killing germs. He sings about saving lives. These ideas sound fun when they are put to music.

The Voice of Experience

People in Niassa like Santos's songs. So do people in other poor places. Singing lets Feliciano dos Santos share his ideas. He hopes his songs can change the world!

Feliciano dos Santos. *"Clean water is a basic human right. Yet so many don't have it. I'm using my music to be the voice of people who have no voice."*

Clean Fun. *Children from Niassa wash their hands at a water pump.*

Playground Songs. *Girls in Sudan jump rope. They sing as they play.*

Rhyming for a Reason

All cultures use music for teaching. Music can make it easy to remember facts. Kids sing songs about numbers. They sing about the days of the week. They sing about seasons and weather.

In some cultures, elders use songs to teach kids. Songs pass traditions along. The songs explain rules. The songs tell kids how to act. The songs tell kids how to stay healthy and safe.

Kids use music when they play. Kids make up songs, steps, and moves to go with games. They sing clapping songs and jump-rope rhymes. They teach songs to other kids. They pass on their own traditions.

Kids often find new music, too. Kids share new tunes, sounds, and beats. They like new ideas they hear.

Always Singing

Music is a wonderful part of every culture. It is a way to share traditions. It tells stories. It teaches ideas and lessons. It reports news. Some music changes with each new singer. Other music stays the same for years and years. No matter where you are or what you do, music will be there, too!

WORDWISE

celebrate: to do something fun for a special reason

history: events that happened in the past

instrument: an object that you use to make music

pattern: repeated or regular group of sounds or motions

song: music that you make with your voice

Music for Festivals. *People celebrate Cinco de Mayo. They dance in special clothes.*

Celebrating!

To **celebrate** special days, people serve favorite foods. They dress up. And people all over the world play music. Music can turn any day into a party.

Many people play special music at family parties. Family songs get passed down from grandparents to kids. Songs travel across the sea. They move from village to town to city. Along the way the words may change. But the traditions stay the same.

People play music on holidays. They sing songs at festivals. They chant prayers. These have been repeated for many, many years. Music is used to show joy and give thanks.

Ending the Day

Parents everywhere sing to fussy babies. A mother may sing to keep a child happy as she works. A father may sing for fun as he cares for children during the day. Parents may sing as their child goes to sleep.

The word *lullaby* comes from the words "lull" and "bye-bye." Lullabies help babies relax. In some cultures, these songs are like prayers. The words tell about keeping children safe. Many families sing bedtime songs. Music can help kids of all ages quiet down at the end of the day.

Goodnight Song. *This mother in Mongolia sings a lullaby to her child.*

Trail Songs. *Cowboys move cows in New Mexico. They sing as they work.*

Singers sailed on ships. They were part of the crew. Singers helped keep sailors cheerful on trips across the sea. Sailors' songs are called sea chanteys. Some chanteys were sung for fun. They helped pass the time while the sailors did boring jobs. Others helped work flow more smoothly. For example, sailors had to pull big ropes. A chantey with a strong beat helped them pull at the same time.

People played horns and pipes to call to animals and to each other.

In Wales, farmers sang plowing songs. Oxen pulled the plow. The steady beat matched the oxen's step. The song's words told the oxen when it was time to turn.

Cowboys in the United States sang songs on cattle drives. Singing helped pass the time. Songs told about the wide-open land. They told about the cowboys' lonely job. Singing kept the cattle calm in the open land. Singing kept the cattle moving on the trail.

Let's wash our hands
Let's wash our hands
For the children to stay healthy
For the uncles to stay healthy
For the mothers to stay healthy
We build latrines

— Feliciano dos Santos

Make Music!

Connect with the world's many music traditions. Then answer these questions.

1 How do people use music to keep their traditions alive?

2 What are some ways people use music when they work?

3 How is music used for celebrations around the world? How does the author compare these traditions?

4 What are Santos's songs about? How do the songs help people?

5 Think about Santos's music. What music in "Music and Culture in Harmony" is it like?